TRANSLATION

A POETRY CHAPBOOK
CONSTANCE PLUMLEY

TRANSLATION © by Constance Plumley, 2017. ALL RIGHTS RESERVED.

First Edition published worldwide by QuickDraw Studios

No part of this book may be reproduced or transmitted in any form or by any means, electronic or mechanical, including photocopying, recording or by any information storage and retrieval system, without written permission from the author, save for small excerpts for review purposes.

This is a work of fiction. Names, characters, businesses, places, events and incidents are either the products of the author's imagination or used in a fictitious manner. Any resemblance to actual persons, living or dead, or actual events is purely coincidental.

For Paul Rogov, who believed in me, who saw in me something beyond the ordinary, this one is for you:

Я люблю тебя всегда.

The Magician

Eyes thrown
like darts
in tender revolt
to our rough-hewn
attempts
at casual frailty.
Nothing,
and no one
can say that
the fingers
at the end
of this flower-veined
hand
did not click the pen
up and down
down and up
again
furtively to aim
for the eyes, the heart
not noting, although
noticing
the crucial stops
between
those two
ticketed destinations
or destinies
come forward
or pull
back, it seems
so inviting
to walk in confident
as a goat

with my transplanted
lambs
heart to some
considerate slaughter
or some
untold bliss.

Tidal

You know, we
know, all of it.

Right now this
may be all and only,

Maybe,
but oh, I'm more a

gypsy moth
than a butterfly,

though the
survivors of the sacrifice

would show
and and tell me different

if they could
rise or speak somehow,

and warm me coldly
up from the ash.

See, this is how
you crash upon me.

If I were to give you any title
it would be Tidal,

Oh, my Aleph,
my one strange syllable,

my letter, my letters,

all of them.

My soul,
and hungers, too.

Translation

It was not his mother tongue
That broke my heart
But the words from his mouth
Not the forests he trudged through
To get here but the currency
He used to stay.

I sit, I drink tea, I speak
To him though he is gone now
Yet was never here to begin with.
I say: Five, six, seven.
Spring, Summer, Autumn, Winter.
And the lesson tonight is this:

I go.
You go.
She goes.
They go.
We will go.

I don't yet know how to say
He returns though I hope he will.
I love his heart and hate his broken eyes
His lovely mouth for saying
I love you and then spitting me out.
Leaving me with foreign words,
Strange idioms,
And disbelief, quiet and sullen as his hands
On guitar strings,
Tears as plentiful as snow on the steppe.

Hands.
Cake.
Love.
Drink.
Dance.
Read.
Speak.

Someday, we will go.

SHEMA

They all fell one by one into the widest sea
imagining there was some vision waiting for them across it,
some piece of peace, or a ring of silence, strung up with lights
save yourself, save me.

They all fell one by one then into the widest sea
imagining your eyes like valleys across it
your hands
like candles and lips like cradles beyond it.

Oh, my dear,
the layers we could shed to fall naked into the water
to be born again and shed
our chaos like burning blue stars
six-pointed, assuredly,
and no map

to the place we might find ourselves,
if in fact we did meet ourselves there
new and free of the burden of history,
some piece of peace, or ring of silence,
strung up with lights
save yourself, save me,
Oh, my dear, my dear
watch me shed my layers
see me.

.

Heavy

My heart was split open
and filled with light,
tumbling Ocean salt water.
I sort through a tangled lineage
with a pearl-handled comb
and miss my companion who dealt
in words and cashed them like currency
every night that I was awake too late
waiting to hear the brush of angel's
wings on my window.

Now I will listen to way numbers speak.
I will untie my tired hands and open them up.
I will cradle the smallest things
lone phrases and a gentle cadence
and look for all the places I can find you
on the map standing under a streetlight
in smoggy midnight Los Angeles
camouflaged in Mink's forest leaves
and tell you all the cities I have yet to visit.
Words tumble out into an empty book
where I write in ash colors

I think I will always be waiting
in that place time stopped and spun into
one moment like that single flower grown in space.
It's true some things are never finished and all
the empty spaces are full of you.

Breath

If you wait the world will
lay on its side and open up
spilling earth and water and
hot jewel-encrusted ore and
we will rise from the ash and concrete.
See, what I want to say is that
the possibilities are infinite
as those first letters from the mouth
of G_d as that one moment
when the depths of your eyes
were contained in a single syllable
and the sound of the waves dangled
from the edge of a divine mouth
waiting patiently to be housed
in the whorls of your ears.

Zen

As long as words
fly defiant and soaked in black
ink from the cage of my heart
there will be poetry.
A poem for you
with your strange elegance
and your sad face,
the way I never wanted
to lose a single moment
or divide our breath
between shores.
It all escapes
me in a whisper
the tears fall
or they don't
it's all inconsistent as weather.
Even now I can
hear a bell in the distance
calling my attention
to the moment just
as it fades
and I close my eyes.

Dig

My own fierce
nature compels
me to dig for fire.
When I ripped out
your heart I was only
looking for the spark,
one lava struck tragedy
sounding like a bell
in the empty gutted
cavern of your chest.

Muse

So,
you gut yourself
like a fish
or a surgeon
with some
precise
bit of death wish
rip out your
heart
a few times
a day, throw
it before
them, the
populace,
the beggars,
the frauds,
the thieves,
yet no one looks
or scoops it up,
because
there's a juggler
around the
street corner
and a whore around
the one after that
and if
you were
to examine the situation
you'd see that
she is prettier in
reality
than you are in the

abstract,
and certainly more honest.

Pattern Recognition

He always
spoke of patterns
in that far off
voice I had come
to know as love,
encompassing, wide
as the ocean;
I never knew how I
shinned like a
beacon in the darkness,
or how his hands
could decipher the day
catching phrases,
forming glyphs of
passage in the
familiar shape
of his lips.

Need

All the empty on the last page. Truncated. Absolute. Absent.

Brilliance tethered with rope to a pack of wolves. I can imagine the cries in hell are quite indistinguishable from the cries of those desperately clawing warmth from the empty. And we think we know. I thought I was free once too, but it was a lie. You wouldn't lie to me would you? Your curious cat. Your blonde salt water train wreck furious and furtive under your sheets. Don't you see? Humiliation has crept into the way I need you. Over time I may evaporate, leaving only a briny tear drop. All the empty between words, and you never thought to ask. Truncated.

Absolute. Absent.

J'adore.

Doe

You are dark
and important
and burn like flowers.
I can't escape the
memory of your voice
and I die as I feign
your touch on my warm skin.
If this is what it
is to be kept
then consider me bound
delicate as a butterfly
and deadly starlet Seconal red
Is it tragedy or
boundless familiarity?
So it is I know
when your breath is out
of pace with your heart.
I think of your eyes
those deep black pools
where I swim and sleep
and wonder if you know
how close you hold me to
your heart.
A doe
who stumbles
wide-eyed to your door
at night
begging entrance
and asylum.

Awakenings

The rising tide is falling fast
down a quiet slope
and somewhere
a boy loses his footing in the snow,

finds a bee a hive
locked in ice
takes it home and
thaws it out.

The rising sun is falling fast
down a loud incline
and somewhere a girl loses everything
she never had,

finds an old hope
locked in ice
takes it to the street
and bakes it in the sun.

The rising dust is falling fast
down a whisper of a rabbit hole
and somewhere someone
a you or an I sits frozen

waiting for someone
to take us home,
take us to the street
and thaw us out,

up from under
warm again.
As we rise from snow
We rise from sleep.

Akimbo

A queer juxtaposition

    supine

a Summertime spent

    in rags

wagging our tongues eager

    as dogs

Lost or newly fallen,

    destitute

or bold, a theory of being

    strung up

alongside overripe fruit from all

    those trees--

verdant and vernal thoughts, the

    seeds of

which we could no sooner

    claim

than we could each other's

    eyes

hearts wide open for an

      eyeful

of the sweetest taste.

Clumsy

Oh you know
that time when
I gutted you
clumsily,
lustily,
like an impatient
surgeon, or
a mute looking
for her lost words.
Nothing said,
"*That heart is his!*"
and so, I left
with it under my coat
to look
after when lonely,
to remind
me of you--
Its quiet cadence
warm at night
under a sallow
moon
that you swore
you could bring
down with
your fists, or lips,
no difference
ultimately
in time or space.
Gasping,
I would always
run after you
and laugh,

tears in my eyes,
dumbstruck
by your beauty.

CURRENT

If I were to strip everything
away
what would be left?
The silence would be
deafening.
I would glow inside of it.
Reduced
to frequency.
An aftershock.

Burnt Season

How the hours unfold
burning the brick buildings down
and screaming children wide awake
crying out the windows and
startling the ghosts who rattle and shake.

Disjointed

It's all in the memory
that curves and bends but never breaks
all the things that fall away
your head floating above your neck
only shadows and moth-eaten lace there
in between.

Haiku

I want pages of lonely girl haiku
the kind you whisper
the spaces in between words
clogged with birds that will
never fly and midnight men
leaving your life and the happiness
they found in your arms
and trains going to the
wrong side of the state.
I want your words to be my armor
because somehow
after all these years
you with your contradictions,
your stupid pride,
your untrammeled lust,
you are still my hero
in a world gone silent as the rush
of wind through leaves.

Eros

The night
you stitched me together
aligning my insides like stars,
tracing my curves and lines like
the strange lunar lineage
your eyes and hands
knit together across the expanse
of my body and my alien face,
that says I don't quite
belong here.

At least my origins
stirred inside
the same
cosmic belly as yours
and when we mingled
as particles and
danced amid the solar swell,
we agreed to land together.

Separated by westward winds,
we traveled apart,
and then came together
in a frozen space,
the night
you sparkled and blinked
and time flew
feathering forward,
a strange bird
in the winter dark.

You came
to lodge some
fine-tuned song in my heart
as we parted,
to come together
again as fast or futile
kisses our notes laid upon
the lips of a
stellar acceleration.

It sounded to some
like fire
and others like wind,
our song,
the night we made it
and stitched the
hole our clean tears
burned in the dirty
velvet sky.
I remember.

Honey

The song of wasps
swarming to sting apples
into rubies.

the French say that women's' teeth
are objects so charming they
should only be seen at the moment of love.
You have seen my teeth.

with you
I am a wolf and I growl
My lips curl back and I snarl
together we bite and are fire kissed

so breasts then are but heavy bitten fruit
apples and honey infused with
memory of stings.

La Nuit

Things have to keep breaking until they're whole. That's what I keep telling myself. The nights blink and flicker and glow at my window. Sometimes I tell myself there's nothing out there. But the city sleeps and whistles and I wonder how it dreams. I fall into the rhythm quietly like a planet finding its orbit. I will carve out a space and live among the delicate chatter in my head. A handful of tickets and nowhere to go. A roller coaster ride in the dark leading nowhere but down. How do we do this? How do we promise to keep living when our hearts break open like deserts and all our songs are lonely?

Pairing

I peel your heart to the core
 where it is wet with honey and salted with tears.
 I savor this mean thing grown tender from touch.
 Every thought a conjure for your face as an upturned card in my deck.
 Your eyes are crossed symbols. We cross deserts and dream the night rabid
 a wolf crying with lust daring to fall and fly though we have no wings.

Precise

You are the surgeon
scalpel poking
at my violin-stringed innards
to strike a chord
to find me
doll like and startled
sitting somewhere too deep inside to
touch

NULL

I can't tell you why
I didn't fall
when I jumped.

I can't tell you why
I inhaled but
I didn't stay high

I can't tell you why
I loved you the
way I wasn't supposed to.

The answers are useless,
the questions are drowned
aren't they?

Jettisoned in the bay
of lost sounds
lonely as your hands are empty.

Silence

O to be
pristine
this & not that
to float
not walk
to sing
and not talk
to hold
silence
sacred as
speech
but
infinitely
more
fragile
in the hand
like moths
and nagasaki dust.

Wave Goodbye

A paper ocean
An Ink Black Sea
Places we'll never go to
and people we'll never be.

Words

Not a poet
Just someone who bleeds
cries, thinks, feels
too much.
The slips and drips through the cracks are what is beautiful.
I never knew I was
until wolves
made a midnight feast
of my marrow.

Identity

Two nights
ago or
was it five days
I tried to wipe
crumbs and
strange
bruises off
my thighs
right after I
found you
and left myself
behind.

Horses

You traveled a dark past, following a stormy horizon, dancing with a fading star---and all the boxes of ashes, and all the blood, all the trees, all the foliage of another place, traveled with you. I flung myself over and over into the sea---setting my heart adrift on a Pacific current, offering my jellied brain to the Atlantic waves. Burying things in dirt, or in sea foam, sometimes suffices. Life can be a heavy thing to bare just by itself, I know. But perhaps there were times that you slept calmly, holding things they couldn't touch---and I held onto my separateness, like a birthday party prize. Some races we don't finish, some horses far outrun our years.

Something Waits

More than anything I miss the feeling of carving out a small space to sit in front of the water. It's easy to imagine being swallowed; a comforting thought rather than a frightening one. Imagine yourself just floating along, seaweed tangling in your hair, buoyed by the salt and the motion of the waves.

Think of a person you lost. They died. They walked away. They vanished. They abandoned.

Maybe one day you might find them, but there's a chance they'd be a different person. There's no guarantee of being recognized, ever, and maybe anonymity mixes with a sort of amnesia and allows us to be braver than our hearts would have us feel.

So, a word for loss and lost things. Too often it's sadness that wins out--- but there can be beauty in the way the wind sweeps away the mandalas we paint with friends and lovers and people we loved who never loved us, or places we visited which we never saw again. They are smooth marbles colored like skies, and oceans, and roses, and cat's eyes, encompassing moments.

It is sometimes comfortable to drift and watch your pale limbs flicker against the back drop of buildings and smog and time. The holes in your memory form a quilt of rough cigarette burns and places where the record skips.

Home is in the space between, meaning weaves in and out of the cracks, sly as a snake and slippery.

We can all feel that something waits; we can all dream of travel.

ABOUT THE AUTHOR

Constance Plumley grew up in San Diego, California, writing poems and attending art school. She is currently employed as an artist's model, and lives in Akron, Ohio with her Calico cat, Schrodinger. Most recently she was published in Red Fez magazine. "Translation" is her first collection.

Made in the USA
Columbia, SC
20 March 2020